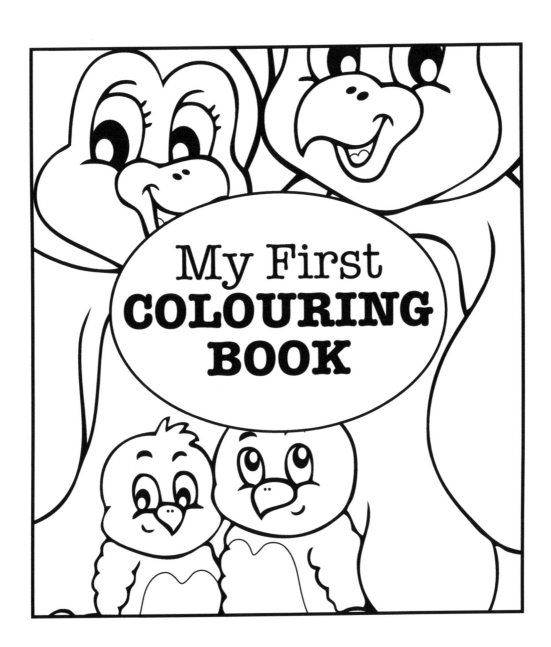

My First COLOURING BOOK

Crazy Colouring For Kids

First published in 2016 by Kyle Craig Publishing

Copyright © 2016 Kyle Craig Publishing

Design: Elizabeth James, Julie Anson, Alison McNicol, Shutterstock, Inc.

ISBN: 978-1-78595-139-8

A CIP record for this book is available from the British Library.

A Kyle Craig Publication

www.kyle-craig.com